HOW TO DRAW
UNDER THE SEA

for kids

ALLI KOCH

Paige Tate & Co.

this book
BELONGS TO

_____

LET'S DRAW!

The nice thing about being an artist is that you can make the rules. Everyone has their own style, which is why your drawings will look different from someone else's. In this book, each sea creature is broken down into steps. My goal is to help you see the simple parts of what may seem like a hard thing to draw.

We will start with the most basic outline or guide and work our way up. You will start to see a pattern with each creature we draw; starting with simple guide lines, then breaking down "C" and "S" shaped lines, and lastly erasing the unneeded lines for the finished look. Don't forget to draw your lines lightly first so it is easier to erase them. My favorite thing to say when drawing is:

If it was perfect, it would not look handmade!

I cannot wait for you to get started. Happy drawing!

TOOLS

The cool thing about art is that you can use any tool you want! Yep, that's right! You are the artist, so feel free to be creative. For this book, let's keep it simple. It's easy to learn using either blank sheets of paper or grid paper.

When you are learning to draw, you really only need a pencil and a good eraser. To follow the step-by-step instructions: draw everything lightly, then go over your lines with whichever tool you would like to use. You can use different pens, markers, colored pencils, or even crayons to add details to your animals.

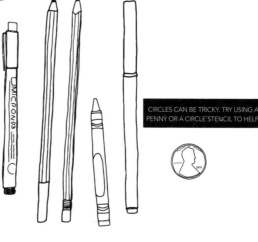

CIRCLES CAN BE TRICKY. TRY USING A PENNY OR A CIRCLE STENCIL TO HELP!

BREAK IT DOWN

Anyone can draw! If you can write your ABCs (which I am pretty sure that you can!), then you can draw everything in this book. Each animal can be broken down into a bunch of "C" and "S" shaped lines. Almost anything that is round is two simple "C" lines put together. An "S" line is for when something has a dip or curvy line.

All of the creatures in this book are broken down into six steps. What you will draw in each step will be a black line; what you have already done will be in gray lines. There are more than 40 creatures in this book for you to learn how to draw. The chapter dividers in this book are also bonus coloring pages that you can color!

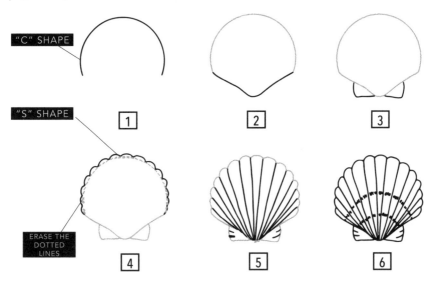

"C" SHAPE

1

2

3

"S" SHAPE

ERASE THE DOTTED LINES

4

5

6

ARCTIC SEA

PENGUIN

The biggest penguin species can grow to be nearly 4 feet tall, while the smallest species only grows to be 13 inches tall!

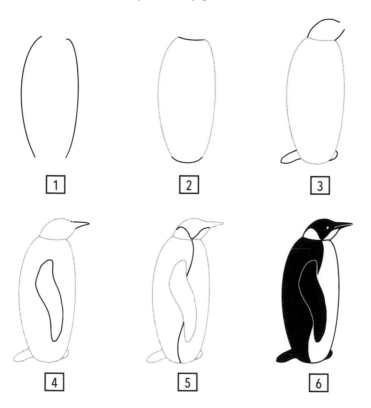

SEAL

Did you know seals and cats have something in common?
They both have whiskers that help them sense their surroundings!

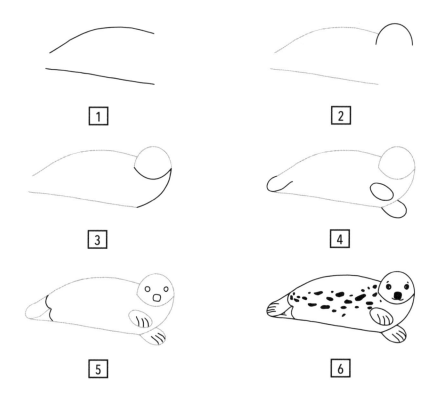

BELUGA WHALE

Beluga whales are the most vocal of all whales—
so much so that they've earned the nickname "canaries of the sea."

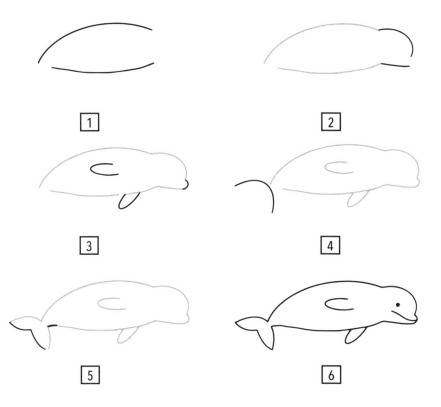

NARWHAL

Narwhals are nicknamed "the unicorns of the sea" because of their large tusks, which can grow to be 8.5 feet long.

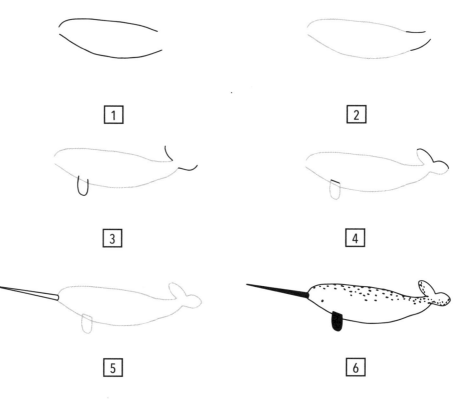

ORCA

Orcas can be found in every ocean.

1

2

3

4

5

6

WALRUS

Weighing as much as 3,000 pounds, walruses stay warm in the winter thanks to their thick layers of blubber.

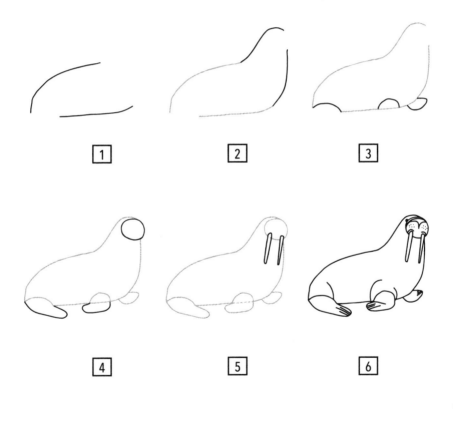

1

2

3

4

5

6

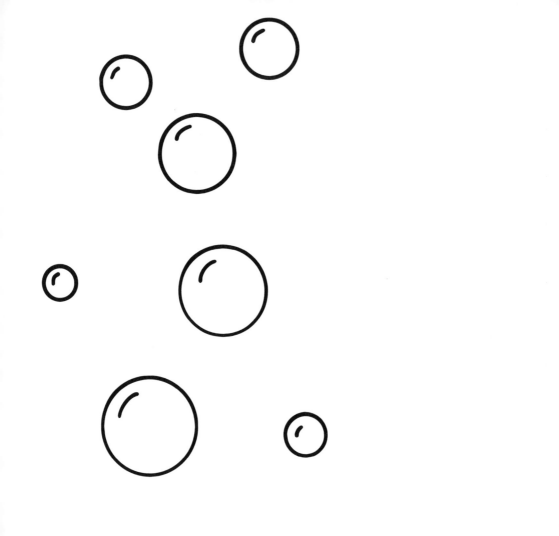

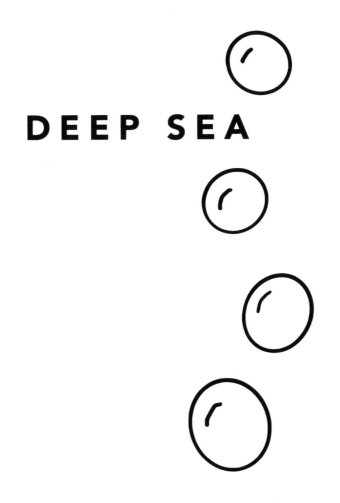

DEEP SEA

HUMPBACK WHALE

Humpback whales can grow up to 60 feet long, weigh up to 80,000 pounds, and their tails can be more than 18 feet wide.

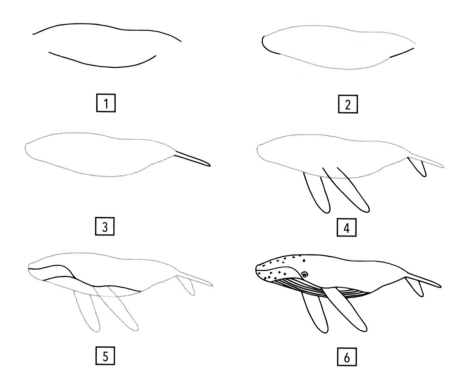

DOLPHIN

Dolphins are great at holding their breath—
they can stay underwater for 15 minutes before needing to resurface for air.

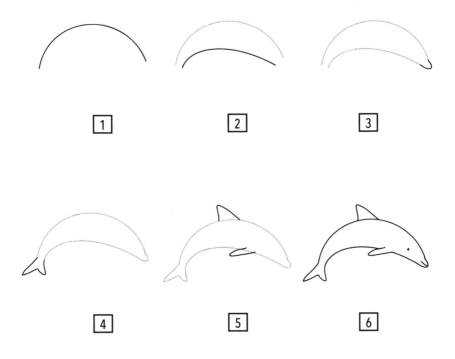

SEA TURTLE

Scientists estimate that sea turtles have been on Earth for 110 million years—
which means they existed with dinosaurs!

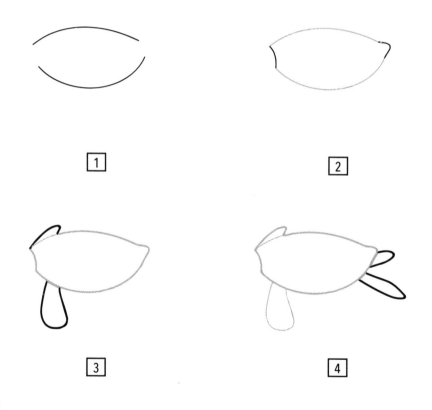

1

2

3

4

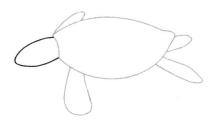

5

6

7

8

SEAHORSE

Seahorses are romantic creatures. They mate for life,
and continue to court each other for the rest of their lives.

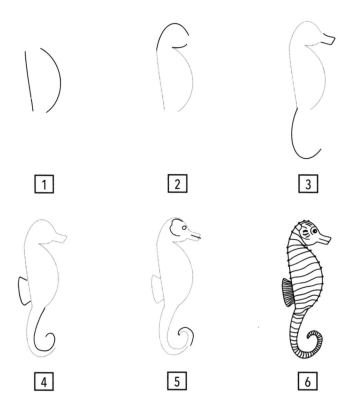

1

2

3

4

5

6

OCTOPUS

Octopuses aren't worried about losing one of their eight tentacles.
If one gets cut off, they can just regrow it!

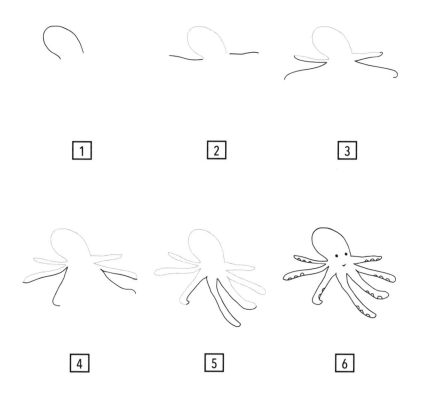

TUNA

Tuna fish can grow to be very big—
the largest tuna ever found weighed 1,500 pounds!

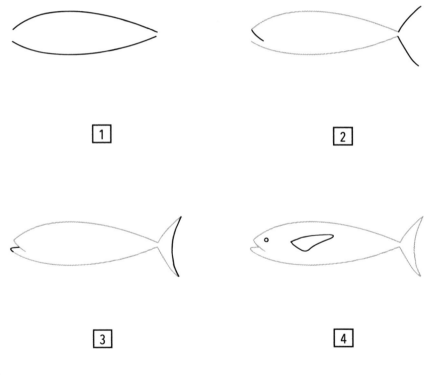

1

2

3

4

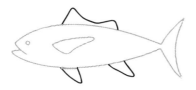

5

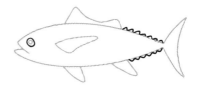

6

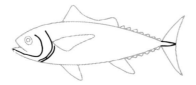

7

8

HAMMERHEAD SHARK

Young hammerhead sharks are called pups—but unlike our furry friends, hammerhead sharks have 360° vision, thanks to their unique head shape.

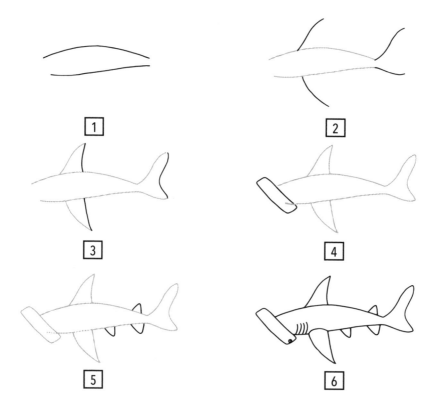

SQUID

Did you know some squids can fly? Some species expel water jets that propel them out of the water, and their fins can flap like bird wings.

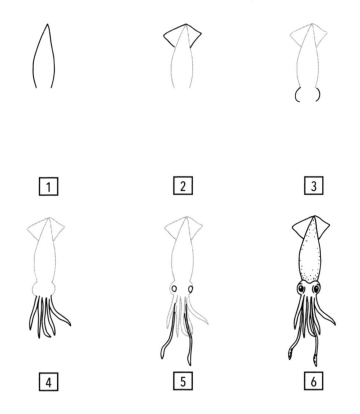

1

2

3

4

5

6

JELLYFISH

Jellyfish don't have a brain, heart, lungs, or blood, making them 98% water!

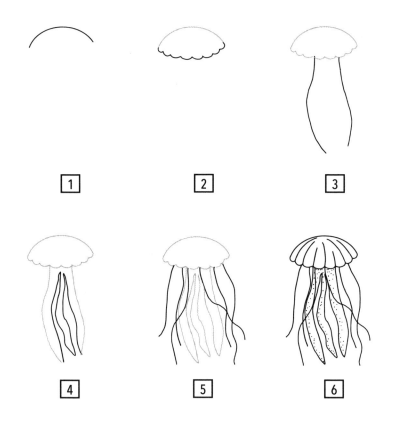

GREAT WHITE SHARK

Before they use their 300 teeth to eat their prey,
great white sharks can use their tongue to taste-test their food.

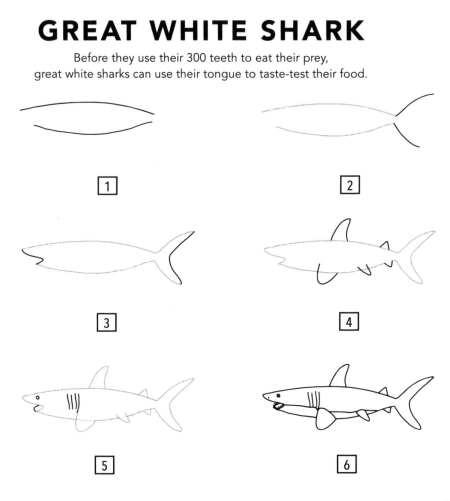

MANATEE

Even though they never leave the water, manatees are more closely related to elephants than they are to other marine creatures.

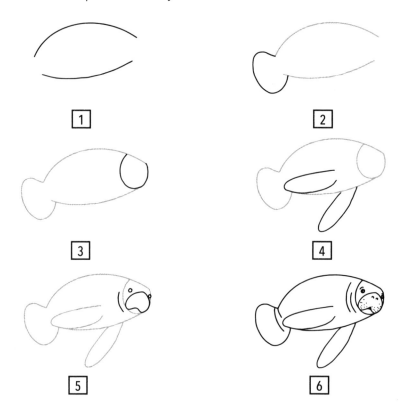

STINGRAY

One of the largest freshwater fish ever documented was a stingray,
and it weighed more than 700 pounds.

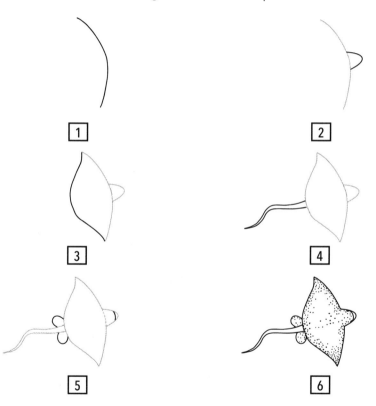

STARFISH

It might look like starfish only have five arms, but in reality, each arm has hundreds of tiny feet that help the starfish move.

CLOWNFISH

Clownfish can be many different colors, including yellow, pink, orange, black, and red.

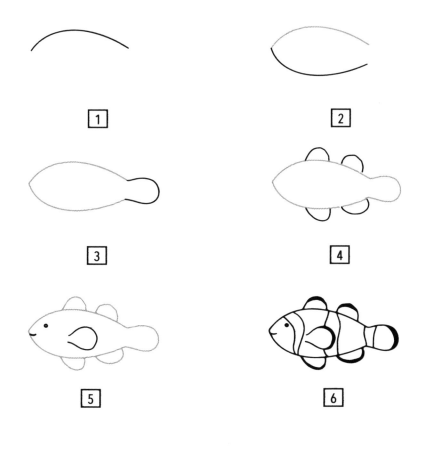

33

MANTA RAY

Manta rays get oxygen from swimming,
which means they constantly have to stay in motion to survive.

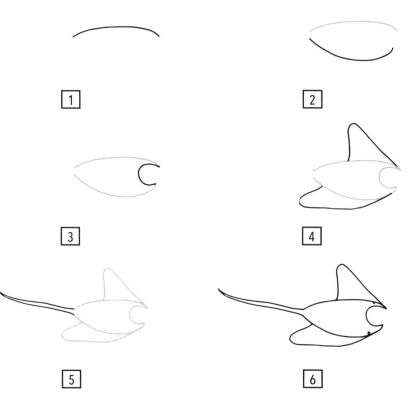

1

2

3

4

5

6

OTTER

Sea otters have the thickest fur of any animal in the world.

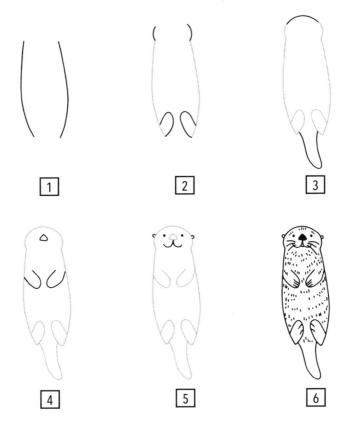

LOBSTER

Lobsters can swim both forward and backward.

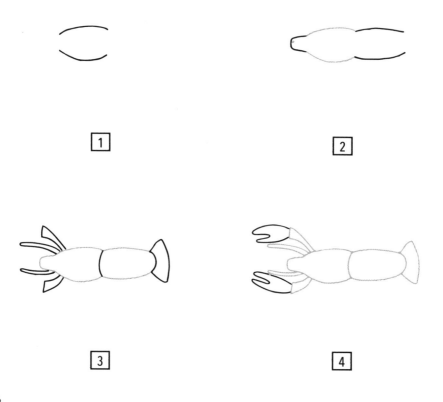

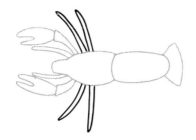

5

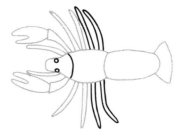

6

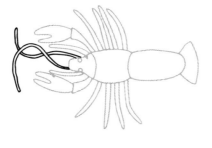

7

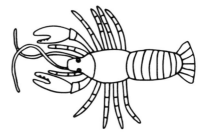

8

SHRIMP

Despite their name, some species of shrimp can grow to be more than a foot long.

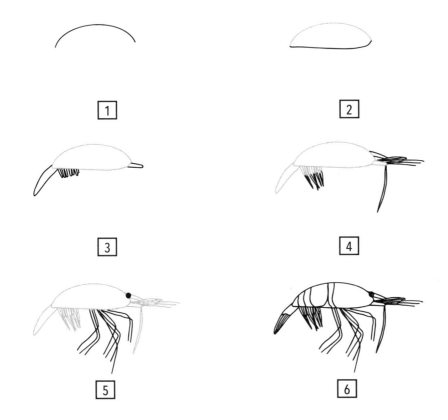

BLUE TANG FISH

Blue tang fish always have a friend nearby!
These fish are often found living in groups of 8-14 other fish.

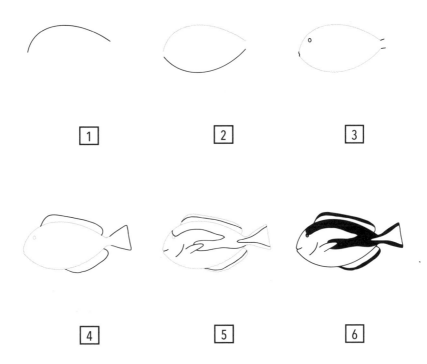

SEA SNAIL

Unsurprisingly, sea snails are one of the slowest creatures in the ocean.

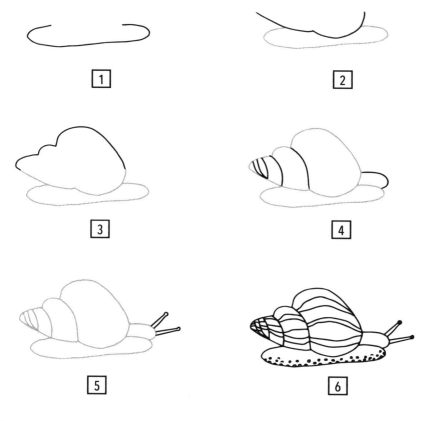

SEA URCHIN

Also called "sea hedgehogs," these spiky creatures don't have a bone in their body.

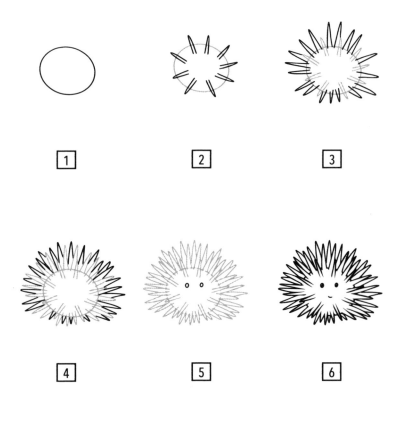

1

2

3

4

5

6

SEA LION

Sea lions got their name because they have loud roars,
and some species can even grow manes!

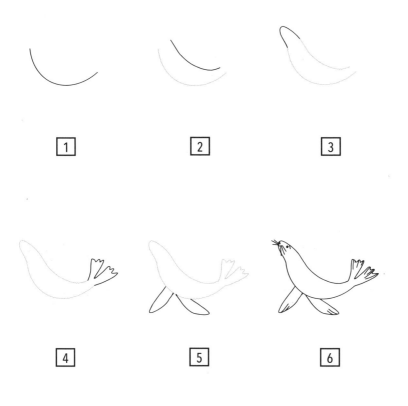

SWORDFISH

Did you know swordfish are one of the fastest fish in the ocean?
Their sword-like bill cuts through water to help them reach up to 60 miles per hour.

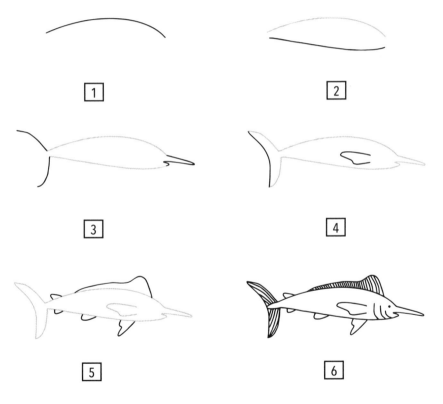

1

2

3

4

5

6

LIONFISH

Lionfish can go up to three months without eating.

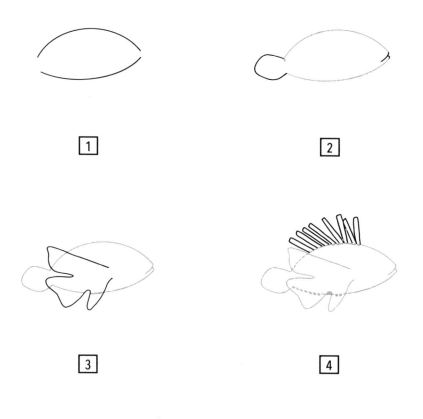

1

2

3

4

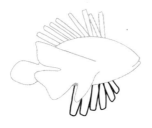

5

6

7

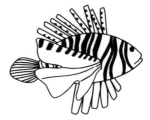

8

EEL

Though they have long bodies, some eels weigh less than half a pound—
making them lighter than this book!

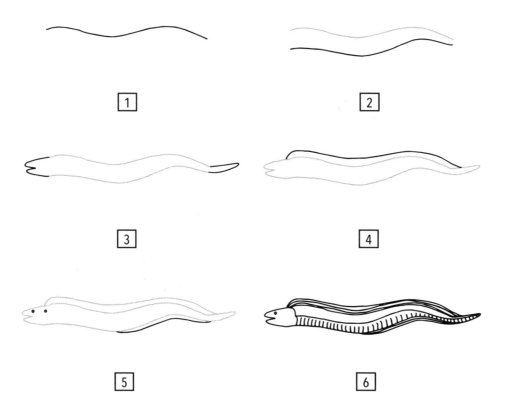

BUTTERFLYFISH

Butterflyfish have a spot on their back that looks like an eye.
This is to confuse predators about which direction a butterflyfish might swim.

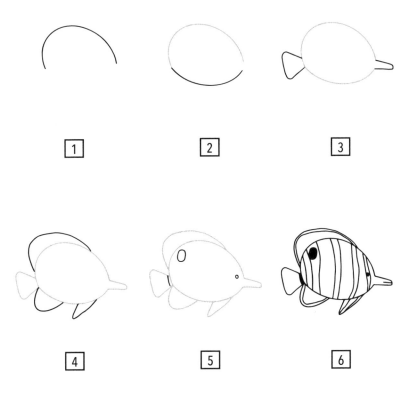

47

SPERM WHALE

Sperm whales have the largest brains of any living animal!

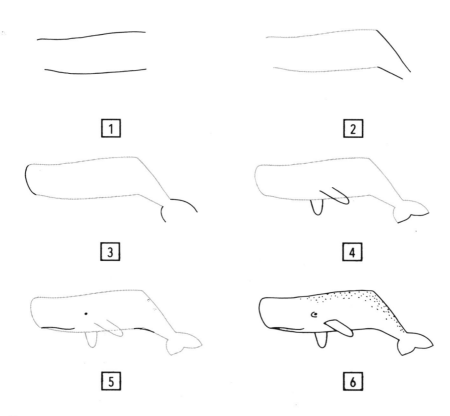

1

2

3

4

5

6

PUFFER FISH

When puffer fish "puff up," they can expand to 2-3 times their normal size.

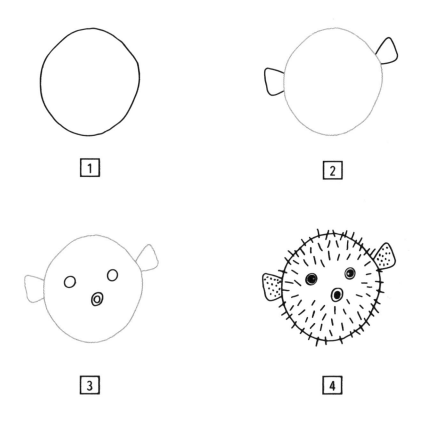

SEA FLOOR

ANGLERFISH

Some anglerfish can produce light from their illicium,
the name for the appendage that dangles from their head. They use this to lure in prey.

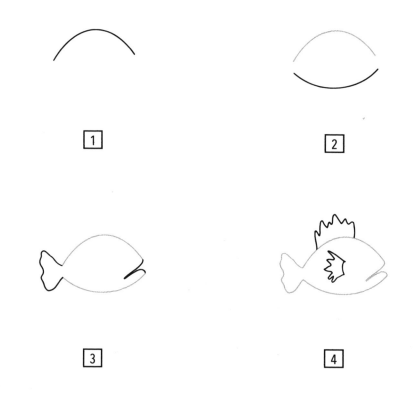

5

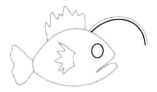

6

7

8

BLUE CRAB

Blue crabs can release over two million eggs at one time!

1

2

3

4

5

6

SHELL

Seashells were used as the first worldwide currency.

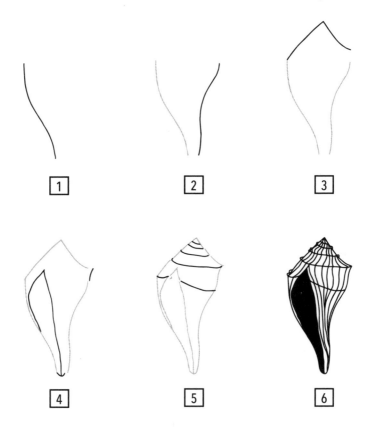

MESSAGE IN A BOTTLE

While people have been putting messages in bottles for centuries, the oldest known message found was written nearly 125 years ago, in 1913!

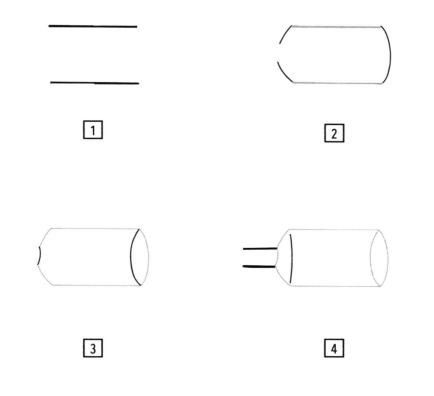

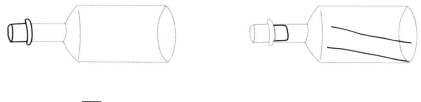

5

6

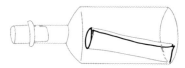

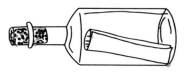

7

8

ANCHOR

Because of their size, large cruise ships have to use anchors that measure between 10-20 feet long and weigh up to 40,000 pounds.

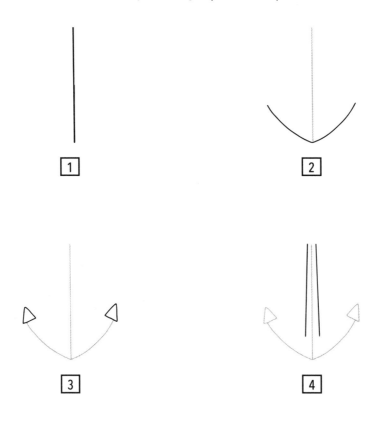

5

6

7

8

SUBMARINE

Early records show that the first submarine was used in 415 BC, although it would have been very different from submarines used today.

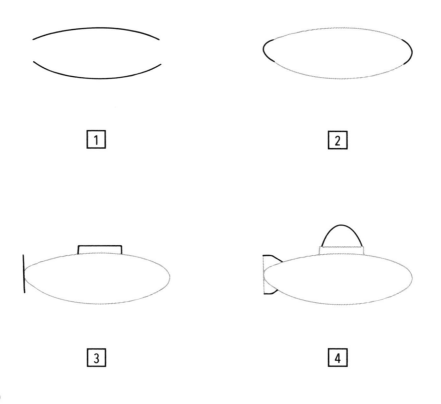

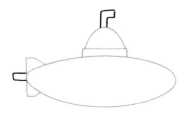

5

6

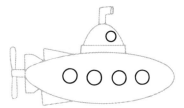

7

8

SOFT CORAL

Did you know? There are hundreds of species of coral, which come in all different shapes, sizes, and colors.

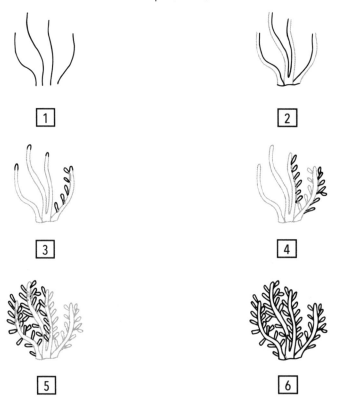

1

2

3

4

5

6

HARD CORAL

Hard corals may seem like rocks due to their hard surface,
but they're technically animals!

| 1 | 2 |

| 3 | 4 |

| 5 | 6 |

VAMPIRE SQUID

The webbing between their tentacles looks like they're wearing a cape,
hence the name "vampire squid."

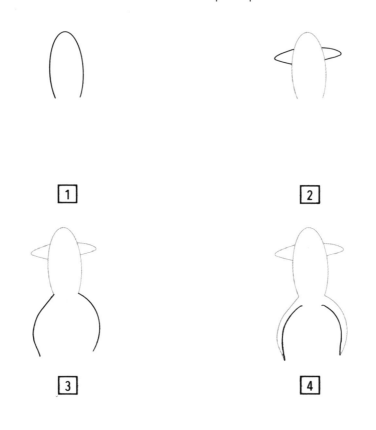

1

2

3

4

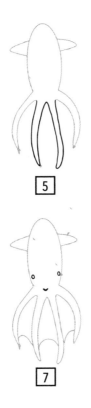

5

6

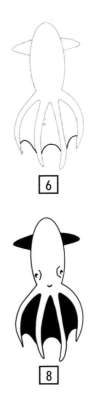

7

8

FLOUNDER

Flounder have a flattened body shape,
which allows them to blend in with the ocean floor.

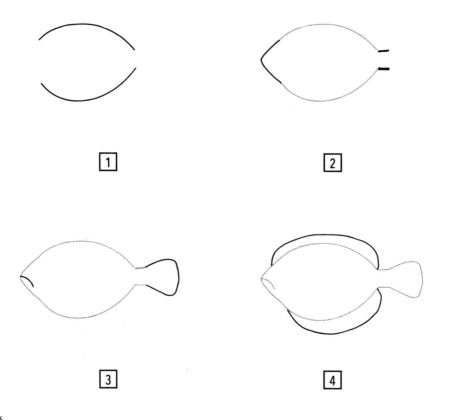

1

2

3

4

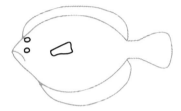

5

6

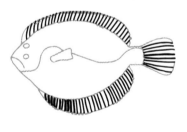

7

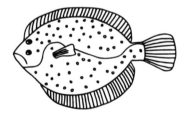

8

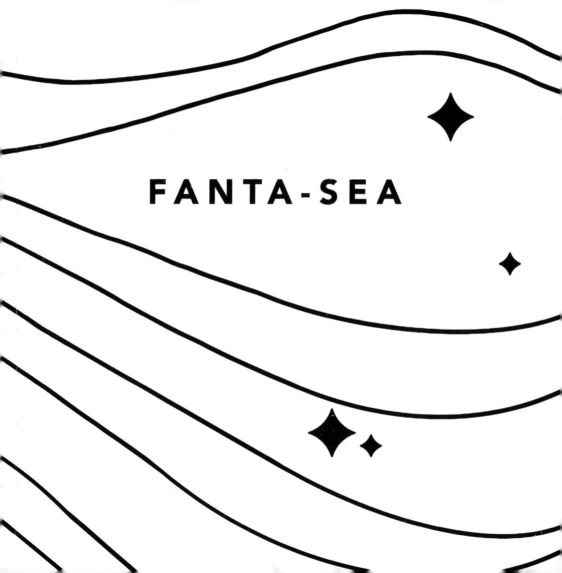

MERMAN

It's believed that, like mermaids, mermen can transform their tails into human legs.

1

2

3

4

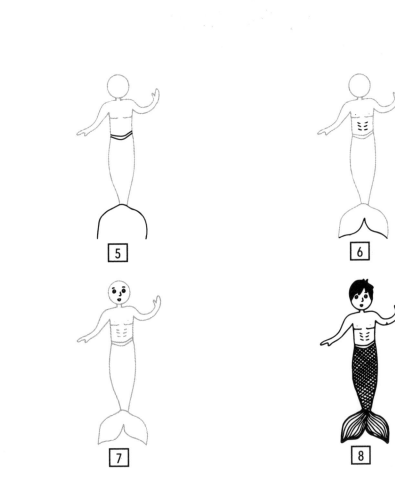

5

6

7

8

MERMAID

The legend of mermaids has long been popular throughout history.
The first believed sighting of a mermaid was in 1000 BC.

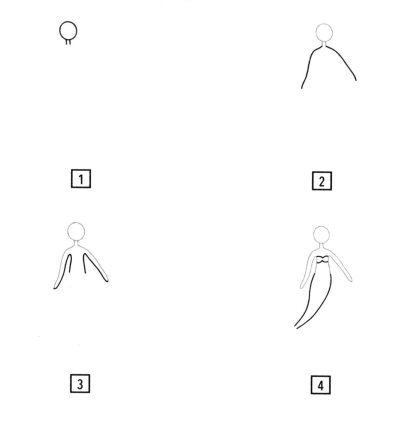

1

2

3

4

5

6

7

8

SEA DRAGON

According to Japanese mythology, sea dragons ruled the sea
and even had the ability to grant wishes!

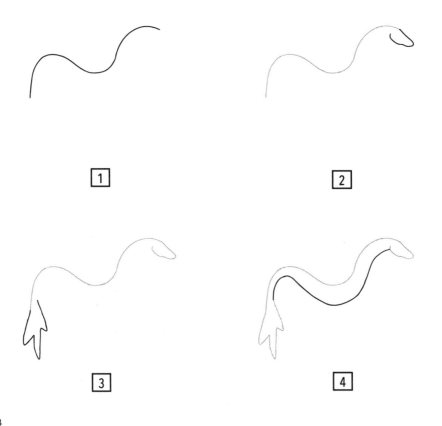

1

2

3

4

5

6

7

8

SHELL WITH PEARL

The pearl is the official birthstone for anyone born in the month of June.

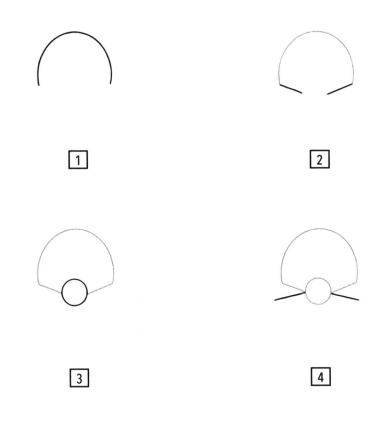

5

6

7

8

BURIED TREASURE

When finding hidden treasure, maps were more valuable than gold for many pirates.

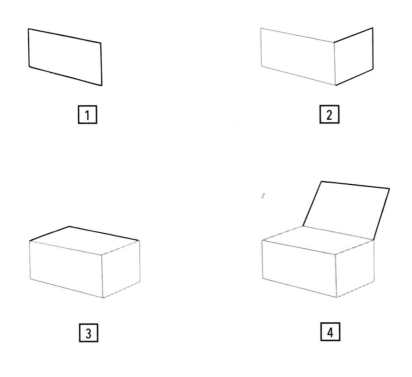

5

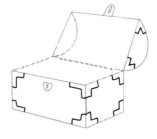

6

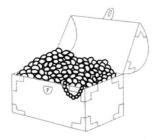

7

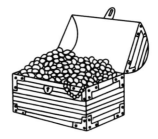

8

About Alli K

NAME: Alli Koch

HOME: Dallas, Texas

BIRTHDAY: March 20, 1991

FAVORITE COLOR: Black

FAVORITE FOOD: Waffle fries and a large sweet tea

JOB: I am a full-time artist! I sell my art online, paint on the side of buildings, and teach others how to draw or be creative

FAVORITE THING: A warm blanket

PETS: I have one cat named Emmie

CAR: Tahoe

FAMILY: Married to my high school sweetheart

FAVORITE ANIMAL: Cats and dolphins

FAVORITE THING TO DO: Playing board games!